Cambridge B1 Preliminary

Writing

Test 10

© 2025 Prosperity Education.
'Cambridge B1 Preliminary' and 'PET' are brands belonging to The Chancellor, Masters and Scholars of the University of Cambridge and are not associated with Prosperity Education or its products.

Part 1

You **must** answer this question.
Write your answer in about **100 words**.

Question 1

Read this email from your Head of Year, Mrs Daniels, and the notes you have made.

From: Head of Year 10
Cc:
Subject: Annual School Trip

Dear Year 10 students,

Thank you!

I am writing to ask you all for suggestions for our next school trip, which this year will be two weeks in July.

In the past, we have taken students to France, Italy, Spain and India. I am prepared to consider any destination for this year's trip, but I will be most interested in places which are suggested by several students.

Kenya — *wild animals*

Let me know where you would like us to go and why you are interested in visiting that country or area.

It would also be helpful if you could find out the average economy airfare to your suggested destination at that time of year.

£350 each, return

Mrs Daniels

Write your **email** to Mrs Daniels using **all the notes**.

Part 1

Part 2

Choose **one** of these questions.
Write your answer in about **100 words**.

Question 2

You see this announcement on your school English-language website.

Articles wanted!
THE WORLD IN 25 YEARS What do you think the world will be like in 25 years? How different will life be? Why **Write an article answering these questions and we will post your work.**

Write your **article**.

Question 3

Your English teacher has asked you to write a story.

Your story must begin with this sentence.

Harry stepped down from his spacecraft and looked around at the black rocks of the planet.

Write your **story**.

Part 2 Question 2

Part 2 Question 3

Answers

Practice Test 1: Writing model answers

These are model answers. Many variations are possible.

Part 1
Question 1: Email
20 marks

Hi Jo,
How are you?
I'm really looking forward to seeing you, too! The last time we met was March, wasn't it?
Yes, I have booked a table for 7 p.m. at a new French restaurant in the centre of town. You have to book early for Saturday at anywhere good. I've been there once before, and the food is delicious. It's much better than the Italian restaurant we went to last time.
On Sunday, if it's nice, we could go to the river. We can hire a boat to go down to Morley and have tea there. How does that sound?

See you soon.

Part 2
Question 2: Article
20 marks

My favourite fi tion is adventure stories which start slowly then speed up to an exciting ending. For a long time, my favourite novel was *Journey to the Centre of the Earth* by Jules Verne, but now I prefer another one of his books. It's called *Around the World in 80 Days*, because there are a lot of different adventures as the hero arrives in different countries.

I don't like science fi tion. I used to like it when I was younger, but most of the stories are not really about the future when you look closely. They just move a normal story onto the Moon or Mars or somewhere. There isn't really any science at all in most of them.

Part 2
Question 3: Story
20 marks

Leah arrived at the house and found the front door open. She was immediately worried. Her grandmother never left her front door open. Leah wondered if she should phone the police, but she would look stupid if her grandmother was OK. So, Leah pushed the door open very slowly. At least, she tried to push it open, but it only moved a little way. She put her head around the door and saw her grandmother lying on the floo . Leah managed to get into the house and, as she was checking her grandmother, the old lady woke up. After a few minutes, she could speak. She said she had gone to the door to look for her cat, slipped and fallen. 'I'll be fin , dear,' she said. 'After a nice cup of tea.'

Practice Test 2: Writing model answers

These are model answers. Many variations are possible.

Part 1
Question 1: Email
20 marks

Dear Mr Collins,

Thank you for your email. I think the idea of a geography quiz is an excellent one. I'm looking forward to it. Here are my three questions, with the answers.
1 What is the population of the United Kingdom? (It's about 68 million.)
2 Where is the United Kingdom? (It's in Western Europe.)
3 What is the capital of England? (It's London.)
I think it would be much more fun if we played in teams. I also think that some of the students might find answering on their own a little bit scary.
With best wishes,

Lucas

Part 2
Question 2: Article
20 marks

My best friend is called Logan. He is the same age as me. I met him on our first day at primary school, when we were both 5. When we got to school, we had to put our coats on hooks. The hooks were in alphabetical order, and Logan's hook was next to mine because his surname begins with the same letter, P. Logan is my best friend because we have the same hobbies and interests. We both like playing football and listening to rock music. We also find the same things funny. We spend most evenings and all weekends together, except when we are away on holiday.

Part 2
Question 3: Story
20 marks

We were crossing the desert when the car suddenly stopped. I asked my father what was wrong with it and he said he didn't know. The temperature was over 35 degrees and as soon as the car stopped, the air conditioning went off. 'Are we far from the town, Dad?' I asked. 'Not far,' my father said, 'but it is too far to walk in this heat.' I was starting to feel extremely worried, when I suddenly saw a big cloud of dust in the distance. A few minutes later, a large lorry appeared out of the dust and the driver stopped. When my father explained the problem, he offered to take us into the town to find a mechanic. We were both very relieved!

Practice Test 3: Writing model answers

These are model answers. Many variations are possible.

Part 1
Question 1: Email
20 marks

Hi, Alice
Yes, it's getting close now, but we're nearly ready. Thanks for getting the perfume. It's her favourite.
I have booked the restaurant. Yes, I did have to try several places before I found one with space. But I think there will be eight of us! Just let me know. I'm sure they can fit in another person if necessary.
I'm afraid I haven't been able to make the cake. Could you possibly buy one instead?
The only other thing is a birthday card. Can you get that, or do you want me to?
Hear from you soon.
Zoe

Part 2
Question 2: Article
20 marks

The most interesting person I have met is my grandmother. She is over 90, but she's still very active. She walks her two dogs for an hour every day in all kinds of weather. I don't know when I first met her, because I was too young to remember. My first memory is when I went to stay with her in her flat in London. I was about eight. Grandma wasn't allowed to have dogs there, but she loved walking, so we went out to the park every day. She played football with me in the park, too. She was quite good! But the most interesting thing about my grandmother are the stories about her life. She has been everywhere and done everything. I hope my life will be as full as hers.

Part 2
Question 3: Story
20 marks

It was getting dark and there was a huge tree across their path. They could probably climb over it, but they had to be careful not to fall in the river. There were crocodiles and snakes in there. After the plane had to make an emergency landing in the jungle, the pilot told everyone not to worry. He had a map of the area, and he said they only had to follow the river down to the town. He said they couldn't get lost. They walked for hours. Then William climbed onto the tree and shouted, 'Look!' At first, they thought he'd seen a leopard or something. But it was the town – finally. He could see the lights in the distance. They were going to be OK.

Practice Test 4: Writing model answers

These are model answers. Many variations are possible.

Part 1
Question 1: Email — 20 marks

Hi, Ben
Yes, I've finished i , too. I thought it was long – did you notice that there are 224 pages! But I thought it was good. No, I haven't read anything by this author either, but maybe I'll read some more of his novels now.
I think the children start to behave badly because there are no rules on the island, but I may be wrong. Let's see what other people say.
The teacher said that we don't have to tell the story because everybody has read it. We have to give our opinion and say what we thought the best bit was.
See you tomorrow.
Arturo

Part 2
Question 2: Article — 20 marks

My favourite hobby is computer games. I played my first game when I   as about eight on a small computer that you held in your hand. You had to shoot at aliens which were coming down the screen at you. You got points for each alien you hit, but they came faster and faster and finally they dest oyed you. Computer games now are much more complicated and exciting. I usually play with a friend, and we play so often that we become experts at any game very quickly. It's a great way to pass the time, but I think it's actually more than that. You learn to think and act quickly, and maybe that's good for real life.

Part 2
Question 3: Story — 20 marks

He heard the terrible noise again. It seemed to be closer this time. He was in the house alone because his parents had gone out to dinner. He hated being alone, but of course he never told them that. Anyway, he knew the noise didn't mean anything. It was an old house and old houses made noises. But there it was again, and even closer this time! He was in his bedroom with his door closed. He couldn't lock it, but the front and back doors were locked … weren't they? Suddenly, the door of his wardrobe slowly opened wide … and his cat jumped out onto the bed. 'Oh, it's YOU!' said the boy, and smiled.

Practice Test 5: Writing model answers

These are model answers. Many variations are possible.

Part 1
Question 1: Email — 20 marks

Dear Ms Marsh

I am very excited about the next school play. I think a musical version of *Oliver Twist* is an excellent idea and I would love to take part.

I hope you will consider me for a large part because of my acting experience. I took the main part in *Treasure Island* last year. The year before, I had a large part in the Narnia story, *Voyage of the Dawn Treader*.

I am happy to sing in the play, because I am the main singer in a rock group I have been in for several years.

I look forward to hearing from you.

Yours faithfully,

James Lewis

Part 2
Question 2: Article — 20 marks

I was going to write that the best teacher I have ever had is my mother, but I think this article should probably be about people who actually work as schoolteachers. In that case, the best teacher is the history teacher that I have at the moment. I like history, but some history teachers are quite boring in my experience. They just give you names of kings and queens, and the dates of battles. But my history teacher this term puts us into the position of the people in history who had to make decisions. That gives us a chance to say what we would have done, and then tells us what happened and why. It's a very interesting way of teaching, and I definitely learn far more this way.

Part 2
Question 3: Story — 20 marks

The wind was getting stronger and pushing the tiny boat out to sea. Sam knew the weather forecast was bad. He began to wonder why he'd agreed to go sailing that afternoon. They had reached the island easily and had a picnic there. It was when Sam and Elliot were halfway home that the storm arrived. The wind was now blowing them away from the harbour. Elliot said, 'OK. We've got to phone for help.' But when Sam looked at his phone, he saw they had no signal. Then he had an idea. 'Can we get back to the island? We can stay there until the storm passes.' 'Brilliant!' said Elliot, and he set sail back to the safety of the island.

Practice Test 6: Writing model answers

These are model answers. Many variations are possible.

Part 1
Question 1: Email
20 marks

Dear Mr Martin,

Thank you for your email. I'm pleased to hear that the fair will be held again this year. I really enjoyed it last year and I think everyone else did, too. I'm looking forward to taking part this time.
I will be working in a group with Vicky Scott, who is in Class 10C, and Harry Smith from 12C. We have decided to call our team 'Waterworks'.
The principle which we will be demonstrating is that water pressure increases with depth. We are already planning how to do our experiment. We're looking forward to discussing it with you.

With best wishes,

Part 2
Question 2: Article
20 marks

My favourite film is actually very old. I have never seen it at the cinema because it hasn't been shown for years. But it is shown on online film channels all the time. It's called *Jurassic Park*, and it's about a scientist who manages to bring dinosaurs back to life. I think the best part is where they see the first dinosaur. When the people first see the monster in a horror film, it's always a difficult scene. It can be disappointing because the monster isn't very scary. But for me, the enormous dinosaur is extremely scary, because this animal actually lived on Earth over 60 million years ago.

Part 2
Question 3: Story
20 marks

My father shouted, 'Get inside – we've got about a minute until it gets here!' I could see the huge column of dust in the distance. A minute? But it was still miles away. My father pulled me back into the house and through to the kitchen, He bent down and pulled a handle in the floor. The cellar! Of course. We went down the ladder into the darkness. My father turned on the light, but suddenly there was a terrific noise, and the light went out. We waited in the cellar for 30 minutes, then climbed back up the ladder. Carefully, my father opened the door and we looked out. The tornado had gone, but … our house had gone, too!

Practice Test 7: Writing model answers

These are model answers. Many variations are possible.

Part 1
Question 1: Email
20 marks

Hi Poppy

Sorry to hear that you've been ill. Are you feeling better now?
Yes, I am in charge of the party. I wish I'd never agreed to it, though! It's been a lot of work, but I'm nearly there now.
Thanks for the offer of help. Ruby is doing the sandwiches and Will is sorting out the drinks. BUT we still need some cakes, so if you could buy them, that would be great. You can spend up to £30. I'll pay you back tomorrow at school.
Thanks again for your offer.

See you soon

Part 2
Question 2: Article
20 marks

I am quite young, so I hope I will have a lot more really good days, and perhaps even a day which is better than my best day so far. But, until now, my best day was my 12th birthday. I have always loved dogs, and I had asked my parents again and again if we could have one. They always said I was too young, and I probably was when I first sta ted asking. But either they got bored with saying 'No' or they thought, 'She's old enough now.' Anyway, on the morning of my 12th birthday, I woke up late because it was a Saturday. My mother came in holding my new best friend – a twelve-week-old puppy.

Part 2
Question 3: Story
20 marks

The alarm hadn't gone off and n w Suzi was late. She couldn't possibly get to school in time for the test. She knew she'd missed her bus when she saw there was nobody at the stop. The next bus came quite quickly, but she was now over 20 minutes late. She jumped off the bus outside the school and ran all the way to the exam room. She was surprised to see the door was open, and when she went in, all the students were talking and laughing. She found the desk with her exam number on. As she sat down, the examiner arrived. 'Sorry I'm late,' he said. 'My alarm didn't go off and I missed   y bus.'

Practice Test 8: Writing model answers

These are model answers. Many variations are possible.

Part 1
Question 1: Email
20 marks

Dear Mr Haynes,
Thank you for your email about the geography project. Could you tell me when the project must be handed in by?
I am working on this project in a group with Mae Green from Class 10A and Ben Simms from 10C. For our topic, we have chosen Weston House. We chose this place because it changed from being the family home of the Westons to being a luxury hotel, and it has now been turned into flats.
I do have one question. Please could you let me know how many words you are expecting for the project?
With best wishes,

Part 2
Question 2: Article
20 marks

I have had different favourite subjects in the past, but at the moment my favourite is biology. I like it because we are looking at climate change, what is causing it and what we can do to reduce it. I don't want to live in a world where the temperature is too high for crops to grow or farm animals to live, or a world where the sea level rises and destroys hundreds of cities on the coast. So, I want to learn all about the subject at school and then go on to study it at university. Then I can go out into the world and make a difference.

Part 2
Question 3: Story
20 marks

It was the day of Oliver's 12th birthday, but he wasn't feeling very excited. His mother had already told him that they couldn't afford the present he wanted – a new mountain bike. She said they might be able to manage it next year. Oliver opened his presents at the breakfast table – a helmet, gloves, knee pads and elbow pads. They were all for mountain biking! 'Aren't you going to put them on?' his father asked. Oliver didn't see the point, but he knew his parents were doing their best. Then his mother called from outside. 'Come here, Ollie.' So he got up slowly and walked out … to see his mother holding a bright red mountain bike.

Practice Test 9: Writing model answers

These are model answers. Many variations are possible.

Part 1
Question 1: Email
20 marks

Hi, Sofi
I'm really sorry to hear that you've been ill. I hope you're feeling better now.
We've already got that perfume, actually. Eva recognised it as one of her favourites, too.
We decided in the end to each give one pound, which means we've got £29 with your money. The perfume was £26, so we were wondering what to do with the rest.
A card is a good idea. Could you get one for up to £3.00 and I'll give you what's left from the class money? We can all sign it on Friday.
See you soon.

Part 2
Question 2: Article
20 marks

My bedroom is at the top of our house – well, in the roof really. It's great being right up there, away from the rest of my noisy family. I used to share a room with my little brother, which was fun at times, but he can be very annoying. That's why I love having my own room now. It's smaller than the room we shared, but of course I've got more space because it's just me. There's a small desk by the window, where I do my homework or just look out the window at the street below. I've got a small television and my computer games in my room. The only thing I don't like about my bedroom is that it's a bit cold!

Part 2
Question 3: Story
20 marks

George was feeling really sad as he put the last few things in his suitcase. They were leaving the house in a few minutes, the house he had grown up in, the house he loved. They were moving miles away because his mother had got a better job in a different city. George had to change schools, and he hated the thought of not seeing his friends very often. His father called him, and he left his room for the last time and got in the car. An hour later, they pulled into the drive of the new house. George saw a boy of his own age standing in the garden of the house next door. 'Hi, and welcome!' he said as George got out of the car.

Model answers

Practice Test 10: Writing model answers

These are model answers. Many variations are possible.

Part 1
Question 1: Email — 20 marks

Dear Mrs Daniels,
Thank you for inviting us to suggest destinations.
I would really like to go to Kenya because I am extremely interested in seeing wild animals in their natural environment. I have been to the city zoo and seen lions and elephants and other animals, but it is not the same. I feel rather sorry for the animals in that situation.
I'm sure a lot of my classmates would also like to go to this destination.
I have researched the airfare, and in July the average cost is around £350 per person for a return flight. There are discounts for large groups of people.
Best wishes,

Part 2
Question 2: Article — 20 marks

I think the world will be completely different in 25 years. Think of how much things have changed in the past 25 years! Personal computers, smart phones and sat nav all mean that our lives are completely different from the lives of our parents when they were young. Social media has also changed the way we communicate.

I think all those things will develop even further in the next 25 years. I'm sure air travel for business will go down because people will have meetings online instead of face-to-face.

Maybe even travel for pleasure may reduce. Companies might develop virtual reality so that you think you are on a beach or up a mountain, when you are really in your living room!

Part 2
Question 3: Story — 20 marks

Harry stepped down from his spacecraft and looked around at the black rocks of the planet. Suddenly, he saw a small cloud of dust in the distance. Did aliens live on this planet? They had seen no sign of that from Earth, but they could only see one side. The cloud came closer and closer, and finally he saw that it was a small vehicle. It came right up to Harry and a figure climbed out. Was it human? Yes! He could just see a human face looking through the plastic of the helmet. 'Welcome to Planet X467,' said a voice from the speaker on the spacesuit. 'I am Russian. We got here before you. Come and visit our city on the dark side of the planet.'

Bonus content

selected from:

Cambridge B2 First

Reading

Test 1

Part 5

You are going to read an extract from a blog in which a man named Hartmann Gumason talks about the World's Strongest Man competition. For questions 31–36, read the text below and decide which answer fits best according to the text. In the separate answer sheet, mark the appropriate answer (A, B, C or D).

Preparing for the World's Strongest Man competition is a demanding process, but it's also a rewarding one. First of all, I have to consume a lot of calories to fuel my training. I usually eat around 8,000 to 10,000 calories per day, relying on a diet that's high in protein-rich foods like lean meat, fish and eggs, carbohydrates and healthy fats. I also have to eat frequently throughout the day to reach my calorie goal, so I'm constantly snacking on things like nuts and berries in between multiple large meals.

Secondly, building up almost super-human strength requires intense weightlifting and functional fitness exercises. I train for several hours a day, six days a week, and I focus on exercises that will help me perform well in the competition. This includes lifting heavy weights.

It's important to take care of your body while training, and I make sure to warm up properly before each workout, stretch regularly and take it easy on the days when I'm feeling particularly tired or sore. At the same time, it's essential to push yourself to reach your goals.

Preparation for the World's Strongest Man competition requires a great deal of dedication, and I've had to give up some of my social life and devote all of my time and energy to training. It can also be difficult to maintain relationships with friends who don't understand the time and dedication required to compete at this level. But I'm lucky, I have a network of people who understand and support my goals.

Training also costs a fortune. There are gym memberships, supplements, and equipment, as well as the high cost of travel from Iceland to many different competition venues and expensive lodging for the competition. I mean, it's great to see the world while I'm competing, but it does come at a price early on, I cut down a lot so I wouldn't miss out. But I have made up my mind to give 100 percent to make it to the competition, and I believe it will be worth it.

Of course, I couldn't do any of this without the support of my sponsors. It's vital to have a solid brand and a strong and constant social media presence. This allows you to showcase your achievements, training and personality to a wider audience, and, for some competitors, attract potential sponsors. I make sure to consistently perform at my best and maintain a positive image, both on and off the competition stage, for the reputation of the sponsors. At the same time, I believe in building and maintaining strong relationships with my sponsors, who I mostly meet at competitions. I keep in touch with them, as, to me, it's crucial to provide regular updates on my training and competition progress, and show my appreciation for their support. By doing this, I am able to keep their interest and ensure that the partnership benefits us both.

If you're curious about being a strongman or preparing for the competition, my advice would be to make up your mind that you're going to commit to the tough training schedule, do your research on the challenges your body will face and consider the costs. You could even start putting some money aside for training or when a competition comes up. Don't forget to share your experiences with your family and friends, and find a supportive community of competitors.

It's not an easy path, but it's incredibly satisfying and the sense of achievement you feel when you step on the competition stage is unmatched. So, go for it, and give it your all!

31 What does Hartmann suggest about his meals?

- **A** He tends to stick to strict mealtimes.
- **B** He has to regularly calculate his calorie intake.
- **C** He has to eat food he doesn't enjoy.
- **D** He eats a varied diet to meet his calorie target.

32 What point about his training does he make in paragraph three?

- **A** That working hard and resting are equally important.
- **B** That training hard can make your body ache.
- **C** That warming up and stretching must be done simultaneously.
- **D** That resting can only happen when not preparing for a competition.

33 What does Hartmann say about his relationships?

- **A** He prefers training to socialising with friends and family.
- **B** He can't have friends because of the demands of his training.
- **C** He thinks that his family struggles to understand the effort his training requires.
- **D** He has a group of people who appreciate his commitment to training.

34 What does Hartmann say about the financial aspects of his lifestyle?

- **A** the travel opportunities are what make the costs worth it.
- **B** he gave up things in the past to help him in the future.
- **C** the accommodation is often the most expensive part.
- **D** he nearly gave up because of rising costs.

35 How does Hartmann feel about his sponsors?

- **A** His sponsors increases the amount of pressure.
- **B** He and his sponsors both see the advantages in their relationship.
- **C** His sponsors require him to provide frequent updates on his training.
- **D** He can only gain good sponsors and deals through social media.

36 Hartmann's main point in the final paragraph about training and competing is that

- **A** it is important to socialise with people with similar interests.
- **B** you have to be physically and mentally strong.
- **C** it is worth doing despite the sacrifices you have to make.
- **D** you need to have enough money before you start competing.

Part 6

You are going to read an extract from an article in which a careers adviser gives advice on choosing a university. Six sentences have been removed. For questions 37–42, read the text below and, in the separate answer sheet, choose from options A–G the sentence that fits each gap. There is one extra sentence that you do not need to use.

Choosing a university

A careers adviser suggests how to choose a university

As a careers adviser, I'm often asked by students about the best way to look for a suitable university course when finishing school. It's a critical decision, and one that can have a significant impact on a person's future, so it's essential to approach the process with careful consideration.

Firstly, I always advise students to look into a variety of courses that interest them but also not to stick to things they know. **37** You might be surprised to find that something that you never thought you'd be interested in could turn out to be a great option for you.

There are subjects available that you might never even have heard of, so it's important to look beyond the school curriculum. **38** You can do anything, and not just the typical subjects you learn at school.

Once you have a list of potential courses, it's time to weigh up the pros and cons of each one. Consider the course content, the reputation of the university, the location and the potential job prospects after graduation. Make a list of these key factors and other things that are most important to you, and use it to evaluate each course on your list.

39 Unless you have a million pounds in the bank, you'll need to consider the cost of tuition, accommodation and other living expenses. How are you going to get home in the holidays? How much is rent in the student halls or rented houses? Think about how you'll pay for everything and what support might be available to you, such as scholarships or student loans. The university will often have a list of potential sources of funding.

As soon as you've reduced your list to a handful of potential courses, it's time to start doing your research. Attend university open days and information sessions, talk to current students and read up on the course content and requirements. **40** The more you know about each course, the institution and the fees, the easier it will be to make an informed decision.

When it comes to making the final decision, it's essential to trust your instincts. If a course feels like a good choice for you, and you can picture yourself enjoying the subject matter and succeeding in the university environment, it's likely that you've made the right choice. **41** You need to make sure you're making the right decision, because it's a big financial commitment.

Finally, don't be afraid to seek guidance and support from others. Talk to your teachers, parents and careers advisers about your options, and get their advice on how to approach the decision-making process. It can be helpful to get an outside perspective and to discuss ideas with someone who has experience in this area.

Overall, looking for a suitable university course when finishing school is a complex process that requires careful consideration and research. **42** By following these steps, you'll be well on your way to finding the perfect course for you and taking the next step towards a bright and fulfilling future.

A   It's important to look into a range of courses, think about the positives and negatives of each one, consider the practicalities and do your research.

B   On the other hand, you may decide that you want to stick to something you already know, such as history, maths, or a foreign language.

C   What about comedy, the science of baking, or oil and gas management, for instance?

D   You could also search YouTube, for example, as it's usually possible to find 'day in the life' videos by students at the university you're considering.

E   It's also crucial to consider the financial practicalities of each course.

F   That way, they can keep an open mind and explore a range of subjects to see what might be a good fit.

G   However, if you have any doubts, it's important to listen to those too.

Part 7

You are going to read a newspaper article about a newspaper article about learning a language. Six sentences have been removed. For questions 43–52, read the text below and, in the separate answer sheet, choose the correct paragraph (A–D).

Learning a language

Four people describe how they feel about learning foreign languages

A **Steve:** I've always been fascinated by foreign languages, and I'm finally learning one on my own! It's challenging, but I'm optimistic that I can do it, and I much prefer it to taking lessons. I've found that the best approach is to build up my skills slowly, starting with the basics and gradually adding more complex concepts. To vary things, I like to listen to music and watch movies in the language that I'm learning. This not only helps me practise my listening skills but also exposes me to new vocabulary, and I get to learn about the culture as well. When I find all the learning too much, I take a quick break to recharge, and usually do something different each time. I find walking outside or going to the gym helps me get back my focus and enthusiasm. To me, learning a new language is a great way to expand your horizons and open up new possibilities for work.

B **Borja:** Taking up a foreign language has been a real struggle for me. I find it hard to note down everything the teacher says, and I'm constantly worried about getting things wrong when I hand in my essays and written assignments. It's difficult to make sense of the grammar rules and vocabulary, and I often feel bored to tears during class. Equally, I find it hard to stay motivated when I feel like I'm not making progress. While some people seem to pick up languages easily, I'm finding it very challenging. I don't think it's something that comes naturally to me. I wish I could appreciate the process more, but it feels like hard work. Despite the difficulties, I know that knowing a foreign language can be an incredibly helpful thing for when I go abroad, and I'm determined to push through.

C **Pallavi:** Learning a foreign language has always been a piece of cake for me because I'm great with technology! If you're struggling to pick up a new language, I have some tips that might help from when I was studying and taking lessons. First, look through online resources and apps that can make learning fun and interactive and make notes if you like doing so. Second, set aside specific time each day to practise, and use the same tools and techniques each time to reinforce your learning. Similarly, absorbing yourself in the language by listening to music, watching movies and speaking with native speakers. Finally, don't be afraid to make mistakes! The more you practise, the better you'll get. Practise every day and keep at it, and before you know it you'll be a fluent speaker! It took me a while, but I got there eventually!

D **Adriana:** Learning a new language is something I have always wanted to take up, so I decided to sign up for a course through work. It's been a great way to get into the language and learn more about the culture. To be honest, it's been tricky but also very rewarding. At first, it was challenging to feel confident and keep up with the pace of the group, although I eventually got there. I find that practising regularly and doing activities outside of class helps me to stay on track. So far, I have learned a lot of new vocabulary and grammar, and I am starting to feel more confident when speaking, even though I still make mistakes. Overall, I think that learning a new language is worthwhile, and I am happy that I decided to give it a try. I still have a long way to go before I can consider myself fluent, but I am excited to continue learning.

Which person:

states that learning a foreign language can be a useful skill for travelling?	43
finds learning a language to be quite straightforward?	44
thinks that learning with others was initially difficult?	45
mentions that they do not have a natural ability for languages?	46
explains that making errors is part of the learning process?	47
thinks that it's essential to develop a routine when learning?	48
suggests learning a new language creates employment opportunities?	49
believes that they will succeed with their self-study?	50
says that extra work in addition to lessons helps them to focus?	51
mentions how they feel about written work?	52

Reading B2 | Ten more tests for the Cambridge First   Test 1

Mark out of 22 ☐

Name _____   Date _____

Part 5   *6 marks*

Mark the appropriate answer (A, B, C or D).

| 0 | A ☐ | B ☐ | C ■ | D ☐ |

31	A ☐	B ☐	C ☐	D ☐		34	A ☐	B ☐	C ☐	D ☐
32	A ☐	B ☐	C ☐	D ☐		35	A ☐	B ☐	C ☐	D ☐
33	A ☐	B ☐	C ☐	D ☐		36	A ☐	B ☐	C ☐	D ☐

Part 6   *6 marks*

Add the appropriate answer (A–G).

| 37 | | 38 | | 39 | |
| 40 | | 41 | | 42 | |

Part 7   *10 marks*

Add the appropriate answer (A, B, C or D).

| 43 | | 44 | | 45 | | 46 | | 47 | |
| 48 | | 49 | | 50 | | 51 | | 52 | |

Cambridge B2 First

Use of English

Test 2

© 2025 Prosperity Education.
'Cambridge B2 First' and 'FCE' are brands belonging to The Chancellor, Masters and Scholars of the University of Cambridge and are not associated with Prosperity Education or its products.

Part 5

You are going to read an extract from an interview in which Sam Godfrey talks about the Young Musician of the Year competition. For questions 31–36, read the text below and decide which answer fits best according to the text. In the separate answer sheet, mark the appropriate answer (A, B, C or D).

My name is Sam Godfrey and I am currently involved in the Young Musician of the Year competition. I first realised that I might have a chance of winning the competition about a year ago when my music teacher and I spoke at a school music festival, and she suggested that I try out for it in front of judges. I was hesitant to apply at first because I knew the competition would be difficult and that the level of talent was going to be extremely high. However, after looking it up online, I decided to try, and I was happy when I found out that I had been selected to compete. It was a great moment when I read the acceptance email; I still can't believe it.

Competing in the Young Musician of the Year competition has been challenging. Honestly, all the other competitors are so good. Every musician here is talented in their own way, and it can be stressful at times to know how to succeed. I have to do everything I can to stand out, and that includes building my brand both online and offline, which I've just begun doing. On the other hand, it's also incredibly inspiring to be surrounded by so much talent and to learn from my peers.

The preparation is hard, but having a routine of sorts definitely helps. It's been a bit of a struggle though, especially since I've been living out of a suitcase for the past few weeks and travelling here, there and everywhere. But I've found ways to stay focused and maintain my routine, even when things get busy. I make time for practice every day, and I always make sure to eat healthily and get enough rest. Additionally, I surround myself with positive people who inspire me.

Winning the competition would be a dream come true. Of course, that is my goal – to take home the grand prize and be crowned the Young Musician of the Year. It would be an incredible achievement and recognition of all the hard work I've put in. But even if that doesn't happen, I want to walk away from this experience having pushed myself to the limits, pleased with myself and the effort I've put in and having grown as a musician. I want to prove to myself and to others that, with hard work and dedication, anything is possible. Whether I win or not, I'll walk away with admiration for every single person that has taken part in this challenging process.

Line 26   It would also be a way for me to share my music with a wider audience and inspire others to go after their passions. Therefore, I hope to use my win as a springboard to help my career progress. I plan to continue writing and performing my original music, and to work with other musicians and artists in the industry. And I want to give back by sharing my experience and offering support to other young musicians.

Ultimately, my objective is to make a meaningful impact on the music world and to be remembered as a talented artist. Winning the Young Musician of the Year competition would be a huge step in the right direction, and I can't wait to see what the future holds.

31 How did the writer become involved with the competition?

  A By attending another event.

  B By watching something online.

  C By asking a friend.

  D By asking his teacher to apply for him.

32 In order to be successful in the competition, the writer needs

  A to have a strong internet presence.

  B to receive an acceptance email.

  C to do everything possible to be noticed.

  D to read plenty of books.

33 What has made the competition difficult for the writer?

  A Not having a schedule.

  B Not eating well.

  C Not sleeping much.

  D Not being based in one place.

34 Winning the competition would make the writer feel

  A relieved.

  B skilled.

  C scared.

  D respected.

35 What does 'springboard' mean in line 26?

  A A problem to an existing solution.

  B Something that requires hope.

  C A starting point from which something develops.

  D Something that requires a crowd.

36 The writer's main goal is to

  A write songs for other musicians and artists.

  B influence the music world in a big way.

  C create a place to share music.

  D become a famous music director.

Part 6

You are going to read a newspaper article in which the success of the Jurassic World movie series is celebrated. Six sentences have been removed. For questions 37–42, read the text below and, in the separate answer sheet, choose from options A–G the sentence that fits each gap. There is one extra sentence that you do not need to use.

A Roaring Success

The Jurassic World movie franchise has been extremely successful since the first film's release in the early 1990s.

The franchise has come up with six movies, each one more thrilling than the last, and has broken free of the traditional monster-movie mould. It owes much of its success to the original book, *Jurassic Park*, written by Michael Crichton in 1990. The novel follows the story of a group of scientists and investors who create a theme park filled with dinosaurs. **37**

The book was a success, but its 1993 cinematic adaptation by Steven Spielberg was iconic.

In the story, the characters try to avoid the dinosaur and escape, but the T-Rex continues to chase them, eventually destroying one of the cars and leaving the characters alone and scared. This scene is famous for the terrifying way in which the T-Rex appears and the impressive special effects that bring the dinosaur to life.

Unsurprisingly, the film was a hit, and it also made a lot of money. **38**

The next films that followed were The Lost World: Jurassic Park (1997) and Jurassic Park III (2001), which similarly feature exciting dinosaur battles and chase scenes that keep viewers on the edge of their seats.

However, the films weren't as successful as the first, so the creators went back to the beginning and early ideas. **39** The film featured larger and more terrifying creatures and was filled with action-packed scenes that left audiences shocked. In one key scene, a storm disables the electric fences and allows the dinosaurs to break free. The T-Rex then attacks the cars carrying the main characters, causing chaos and destruction.

The success of the movie prompted the filmmakers to make a follow-up, and in 2018, Jurassic World: Fallen Kingdom arrived in cinemas. **40**

The movie was a hit with fans, and it made over a billion dollars worldwide. The latest film, Jurassic World: Dominion, ends with dinosaurs living peacefully alongside real-world animals.

What makes the Jurassic World films stand out from other monster movies is its ability to create creatures that feel real, despite their prehistoric origins. **41**

In conclusion, the Jurassic World movie franchise has basically set the standard for modern monster movies. **42** Whether you're a long-term fan of the original Jurassic Park or a newcomer to the franchise, there's something for everyone in the Jurassic World.

A Its impact on pop culture will undoubtedly continue to entertain readers and movie lovers for generations to come.

B The filmmakers have used new technology to create creatures that look and move like real dinosaurs, making the movies feel even more fascinating.

C However, this time, the risks were higher – audiences were used to the latest technology so the special effects had to be better than ever before

D The scientific accuracy and attention to detail made it fascinating for both dinosaur enthusiasts and sci-fi fans, making it an instant hit.

E Therefore, it's no surprise that the franchise is so popular.

F Then there were the books, board games, toys and video games, all of which made even more money.

G After a break, the franchise returned with the movie Jurassic World, which ended up being an even bigger hit than the ones before.

Part 7

You are going to read an article in which four people talk about living on an island. Six sentences have been removed. For questions 43–52, read the text below and, in the separate answer sheet, choose the correct paragraph (A–D).

Island life in Scotland

A **Marta:** As a young au pair living on the Isle of Island, this small island in Scotland is simply breath-taking. Compared to my hometown, Islay is a relaxing place, surrounded by stunning natural landscapes. I am constantly amazed by the beauty of this island (when it's not pouring down, of course!) and I feel incredibly grateful to have had the opportunity to live here. Living in a foreign country has definitely been a challenge, but I am so glad that I decided to come here and make this huge change in my life. I signed up for the au pair program as a way to experience a different culture and way of life, and I have not been disappointed. I know that I need to leave soon and return to the real world, but this experience has taught me so much about myself. I will always look back on my time on Islay with fondness and appreciation.

B **Brian:** My wife and I decided to move from the hustle and bustle of life in Glasgow in Scotland to the quiet island of Mull, in the north of the country. We were both feeling stressed, and we knew we needed a change. The demands of the 9–5 were tough, and we needed to find a way to calm down and enjoy life again. However, the move wasn't straightforward. However, the move wasn't straightforward. First of all, we had to cut down on our expenses in order to make this move happen. We knew that we would be paid little compared to our previous salaries, but we were willing to take that chance in order to have a better quality of life. But it was worth it! Life on Mull is much more relaxed, and we have time to appreciate the small things in life and to enjoy the beauty of nature. We have also made some amazing new friends of different ages in the local community.

C **Cameron:** I have always lived on the Isle of Skye, and could never imagine living anywhere else. Sometimes, people suggest that I should consider moving to a bigger city for more job opportunities and a high salary. But the truth is that I couldn't turn down the natural beauty and calmness that Skye provides. Besides, I have been fortunate enough to have found a job that I enjoy and which I can do from home. Obviously, if circumstances change and my job suddenly requires me to travel then I might have to consider leaving, but Skye will always hold a special place in my heart and I know I would be a regular visitor if I did leave. I love hiking and taking long walks, and the island offers stunning views that I know it would take me far longer to find on the mainland. In addition, the sense of 'family' here is incredibly special. Everyone knows each other, and there is a strong support system that is very rare elsewhere. I am grateful to have grown up on this island.

D **Colin:** I live on the small island of Iona, but, to be honest, I can't wait to move away. Don't get me wrong, Iona is beautiful place. But there is not a lot to do for youngsters. Believe me: if you've seen one visitor centre, you've seen them all! I'm still young, so I have to wait a few more years yet, but as soon as I'm old enough I'm moving, maybe to a different country! Some people advise against leaving the island, saying that I'll miss the small community and how quiet life is (I definitely won't!). I feel ready for something new. I've been looking for jobs where I can be a small fish in a big pond for a change. I want to experience new things, meet new people and feel as free as a bird.

Which person:

says that they are tired of seeing the same thing more than once? 43 ☐

compares where they live to another country? 44 ☐

refers to the wet weather? 45 ☐

believes that they would return to visit if they moved away? 46 ☐

mentions earning less money than before? 47 ☐

suggests that they want something more exciting to happen to them? 48 ☐

says that they used to be worried and anxious? 49 ☐

suggests that they don't have much time left on their island? 50 ☐

states that they want to see the rest of the world? 51 ☐

explains how the community is refreshingly different from most places? 52 ☐

Reading B2 | Ten more tests for the Cambridge First   Test 2

Mark out of 22 ☐

Name _____   Date _____

Part 5   *6 marks*

Mark the appropriate answer (A, B, C or D).

| 0 | A | B | **C** | D |

31	A	B	C	D		34	A	B	C	D
32	A	B	C	D		35	A	B	C	D
33	A	B	C	D		36	A	B	C	D

Part 6   *6 marks*

Add the appropriate answer (A–G).

| 37 | | 38 | | 39 | |
| 40 | | 41 | | 42 | |

Part 7   *10 marks*

Add the appropriate answer (A, B, C or D).

| 43 | | 44 | | 45 | | 46 | | 47 | |
| 48 | | 49 | | 50 | | 51 | | 52 | |